Contents

 KU-111-476

Any words appearing in the text in bold, **like this**, are explained in the Glossary. You can also look out for them in the Star words box at the bottom of each page.

WANDSWORTH LIBRARY SERVICE

Doing it all

Some people are famous for their acting skills. Some are famous for their dancing ability. Others are famous for their musical talent. It is not often that someone becomes famous as an actor, dancer and singer. Yet Jennifer Lopez (or J. Lo, as she is often called) has done just that.

J. Lo did not become a star overnight. It took hard work, **ambition** and dedication.

ALL ABOUT J. LO

Full name: Jennifer Lopez
Also known as: J. Lo, Jenny
Born: 24 July 1970
Place of birth: Castle Hill, the Bronx, New York City, USA
Family: David (father), Guadalupe (mother), Leslie (elder sister), Lynda (younger sister)
Height: 5' 6" (1.68 metres)
Religion: Catholic
Married: Ojani Noa (1997), Cris Judd (2001), Marc Anthony (2004)
Big break: Appearing as a dancer on the *In Living Color* television show in 1991
First major film: *Selena* (1997)
First album: *On the 6* (1999)
Other interests: Owns a production company, a restaurant, a nightclub and has her own brand of clothing and perfume

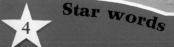
Star words

ambition having something you want to achieve
strive work very hard

She is one of the most famous and most wealthy women in the world. She continues to **strive** for even greater success.

" From the age of five, I wanted to be a celebrity. "

What's in a name?

Jennifer Lopez has many talents and many names. She is often known as J. Lo – a name suggested by her fans. Some people call her La Lopez. However, her friends just call her Jenny.

J. Lo's performance at the MTV Europe awards in 2000 showed that she had star quality.

Find out later

Which film gained J. Lo two best actress award **nominations**?

Which future husband did J. Lo meet making her music video 'My love don't cost a thing'?

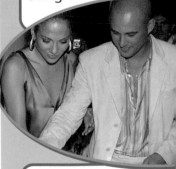

Why did J. Lo name her first album *On the 6*?

The famous fashion designer Ralph Lauren grew up in the Bronx.

Jenny from the block

Jennifer Lopez grew up far away from the glamour of Hollywood. Her parents came from Puerto Rico. This is an island in the Caribbean Sea. Later they moved to the Bronx. This is an area of New York City. Jennifer and her two sisters were born there.

The multicultural Bronx

More than one million people live in the Bronx. There is a wide range of **cultures** there. The population is about one third Hispanic American, like J. Lo. One third is African American. One third is Asian and white. More than a quarter of people in the Bronx are Puerto Rican.

★ ★ ★ ★ ★ ★ ★ ★ ★ ★ ★

Star-studded Bronx

Many famous people grew up in the Bronx. Actor Tony Curtis, pop star Billy Joel, film **director** Stanley Kubrick and fashion designers Calvin Klein and Ralph Lauren all lived there.

★ ★ ★ ★ ★ ★ ★ ★ ★ ★ ★

Break-dancing and hip-hop started in the Bronx.

6

Star words

cultures people from different countries and races
director person in charge of making a film

Star fact

When she was 13, Jennifer was in a car crash. She was not badly hurt, although she did break her nose. Jennifer has no plans for surgery – she likes her nose!

J. Lo's sisters

Jennifer's younger sister, Lynda, is a TV presenter. She worked as co-host on VH1's *The Daily One*. Her elder sister, Leslie, is a music teacher. She loves to sing **opera** music in her spare time.

A musical background

> The Bronx, for me, wasn't tough at all. It was the only thing I knew, so for me it was normal.

The Bronx has a reputation for being rough, tough and violent. It is also well known for its musical history. Many types of music and dance began there. These include **salsa** and breakdancing. In the 1970s, hip-hop also became popular. As soon as she heard it, Jennifer loved this type of music.

J. Lo's sister Lynda also works in showbiz.

J. Lo's roots

Jennifer is proud of her Puerto Rican background. She is proud of coming from the Bronx, too. This has helped her to become who she is. Her song 'Jenny from the block' says: 'No matter where I go, I know where I came from – from the Bronx!'

salsa type of Latin-American music and dance

Starting out

West Side Story

J. Lo's favourite film is *West Side Story*. It is based on *Romeo and Juliet*. She says that she's seen the musical more than a hundred times. It tells the story of rival gangs in New York City in the 1950s. The Jets are American and the Sharks are Puerto Rican.

J. Lo has entertained people since she was five years old. Her parents saw how keen she was to perform. They sent Jennifer to dance classes at the Kips Bay Boys and Girls Club. She learned ballet, jazz and **flamenco**.

A hard worker

J. Lo went to dance classes most days after school. She often stayed late to ask questions or to help other pupils. She always wanted to learn more dance routines and more parts. At the weekend, she travelled into Manhattan for extra ballet lessons. Manhattan is another area of New York City.

J. Lo loved to learn all types of dance, especially ballet.

> I always knew that Jennifer would have a great future. (J. Lo's mum)

Goodbye to law

J. Lo's parents wanted their daughter to study law. Then she would have a good and well-paid job. Jennifer had different ideas. She did not want to be a lawyer. She wanted to be famous.

A scene from *West Side Story*.

Star words   flamenco lively type of Spanish dancing
routine set of practised dance moves

Leaving home

J. Lo's parents were not pleased that Jennifer wanted to be a dancer. Her mind was made up, though. She left home in order to follow her dream. Soon she won an **audition** to study at a dance studio. Later, she went on to tour Europe with a stage show. Now she was really on her way!

Star fact

When she was 15, J. Lo was sacked from a New York jeans shop – for dancing too much!

On the stage

J. Lo has always loved musicals. She first appeared on stage in a drama-club production of *My Fair Lady*. Later, she was in a high-school performance of *Godspell*.

J. Lo returned to her old dance school for a live performance in 2002.

Big break

J. Lo had her first big break in 1991. She won a dance contest to become one of the Fly Girls. The Fly Girls were dancers on a US television comedy show called *In Living Color*. The popular show got J. Lo important **publicity**. She was on the show for two seasons. Then she was ready for her next challenge.

Jim Carrey appeared in *In Living Color* from 1990 to 1993.

★ ★ ★ ★ ★ ★ ★ ★ ★ ★ ★

Jim Carrey

Actor Jim Carrey started out on *In Living Color*, too. He has starred in popular films such as *The Mask*, *Ace Ventura: Pet Detective* and *Bruce Almighty*.

★ ★ ★ ★ ★ ★ ★ ★ ★ ★ ★

Not just a dancer

J. Lo wanted success as an actor as well as a dancer. She won **roles** in television **sit-coms** and dramas. Then she started getting parts in films. By 1997, she had acted with some big stars.

" Selena taught me that we have to live each moment as though it's our last. "

J. Lo was paid US$1 million for *Selena*.

Star words

publicity when someone is noticed by the public
role part that an actor plays in a film, play or television show

J.Lo's co-stars at this time included Woody Harrelson, Wesley Snipes, Robin Williams and Jack Nicholson.

Selena

Jennifer needed a really big film to make her famous. That film was *Selena*. J. Lo starred as Selena. This was a demanding role.

★ Star fact

In 1998, Jennifer Lopez was **nominated** for two best actress awards for her role in *Selena*.

Careful research

J. Lo made sure that she knew as much about the real Selena as possible before filming began. She studied videos to learn how the pop star had moved, sung and danced. She even lived with Selena's family for a while.

J. Lo enjoying the Golden Globe awards in 1998.

The real Selena

Selena told the true story of Selena Quintanilla Pérez. She was a famous Mexican-American pop star. Selena was shot dead by the president of her own fan club. She was only 23 when she died.

The real Selena. She was talented and **ambitious**, just like J. Lo.

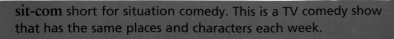
sit-com short for situation comedy. This is a TV comedy show that has the same places and characters each week.

11

Getting into music

J. Lo trained as a dancer and singer, appearing in musicals when she was younger. Acting in *Selena* made her remember how much she loved music. Once filming was over, Jennifer made plans to record her own music.

" There's nothing like singing in front of an audience. "

For J. Lo, the sky's the limit!

The record deal

Many of the major record companies were keen to work with Jennifer. The companies offered better and better deals in return for releasing J. Lo's music. Sony Music made the best offer and signed Jennifer to their Work Group record label.

J. Lo's fans loved her debut album.

Train to success

J. Lo's first album – *On the 6* – was named after the subway train she took into Manhattan for classes and **auditions** when she was a girl.

Star words

produced when a song is produced, this includes arranging and mixing the music

Chart-topping success

In May 1999, J. Lo's first single was released. 'If you had my love' received a huge amount of **publicity**. It was **produced** by top musicians. The video was made by an award-winning **director**. J. Lo made many personal appearances to **promote** this single.

Going platinum

All the hard work paid off. 'If you had my love' topped the US Billboard pop chart. J. Lo's **debut** album, *On the 6*, was released a week later. Both the single and the album went platinum. This meant that they had each sold more than a million copies.

Madonna is one of the most successful musicians of all time.

Music and films

It is rare to succeed in both films and music. Madonna, for example, has tried acting, but is best known for her music.

promote tell people about a new product
debut someone's first appearance in a new role

Films

★ ★ ★ ★ ★ ★ ★ ★ ★ ★

Audition time

Jennifer says: 'The real work comes when you're looking for a job... reading scripts, going on auditions.'

★ ★ ★ ★ ★ ★ ★ ★ ★ ★

J. Lo trained hard for her role in *Enough*.

Jennifer puts her heart and soul into performing, whether she is singing or acting. She has never been afraid to go for **auditions** for the **roles** that she wants. She competed with 20,000 actresses for the part of Selena. She had to audition for her part in *Out of Sight* (1998). She beat several famous Hollywood actresses to come out on top.

❝ I never thought about being a Latina actress, I thought about being an actress. ❞

Star words martial arts types of self-defence or attack, such as judo or karate

14

J. Lo played a policewoman in *Money Train*.

Getting ready

Jennifer spends a lot of time researching her roles. She makes sure she knows exactly how her character would speak and behave. Jennifer prepared for her role in *Enough* by training in **martial arts**. When she played a police officer in *Money Train*, she talked to women from the police force.

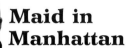

Maid in Manhattan

There are similarities between J. Lo and the character she plays in *Maid in Manhattan*. Marisa Ventura is an **ambitious** woman from the Bronx. She dreams of a better future and works hard to achieve it. This is a role that Jennifer must have enjoyed playing!

J. Lo as her character Marisa Ventura in *Maid in Manhattan*.

Not typecast

J. Lo does not want to be **typecast** as a Puerto Rican. She does not want just to play typical Hispanic women. She wants to be able to play any role. She has a strong personality. She has persuaded **directors** to give her the chance to play different **roles**.

typecast when an actor is given very similar roles to play, over and over again

15

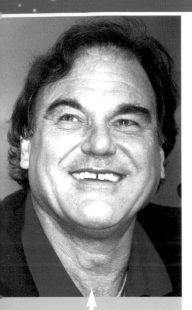

Different roles

J. Lo tries to play different types of **roles**. She has played a police officer, a teacher, a Cuban **immigrant**, a singer, a wedding planner, a killer and a maid.

On set

J. Lo is professional. She works hard to achieve the best result. Many of J. Lo's co-stars have said how much they enjoyed working with her.

> She was an absolute pleasure to work with.
> (Director Oliver Stone)

Oliver Stone directed Jennifer in the film *U-Turn*.

★ ★ ★ ★ ★ ★ ★ ★ ★

The director

The **director** is one of the most important people involved in a film. The director tells the camera crew, the actors and everyone else on **set** what to do.

★ ★ ★ ★ ★ ★ ★ ★ ★

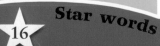

Star words   set part of a film studio where a film is shot

On location

Films can take months to shoot. Some films are shot **on location** in faraway places. This means that the actors have to live away from home. J. Lo has spent time in Brazil, Mexico, California and her home town of New York City while filming.

Audition time

Actors have to be ready for anything. Jennifer starred in the film *Out of Sight* with George Clooney. In one scene, Jennifer is trapped in a car boot with her co-star. When she **auditioned** for the film, she and George acted this scene while squeezed together on a leather couch!

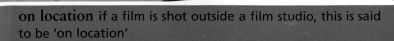

J. Lo and co-star Ralph Fiennes filming *Maid in Manhattan*. This scene was shot on location in Central Park, New York.

★ ★ ★ ★ ★ ★ ★ ★ ★ ★ ★

A tiny role

J. Lo starred in one film as an ant! She provided the voice for Azteca in the computer-animated film *Antz*.

★ ★ ★ ★ ★ ★ ★ ★ ★ ★ ★

J. Lo played the voice of Azteca in *Antz*.

Music

This is Me... Then

Jennifer's fourth album is called *This is Me... Then*. She describes it as 'a road trip, a family vacation, a reunion, a wedding, a birthday and a night on the town, all in one'.

'I'm gonna be alright' was a hit from the album *J. Lo*. The video was filmed in New York City.

Star words

unique one of a kind
compilation CD that includes tracks from different sources

J. Lo's Hispanic roots and Bronx upbringing help to make her music **unique**. Her music is a mixture of hip-hop, Latin and pop. This appeals to a large audience. J. Lo works with different **producers** to try out new musical styles. This is something a lot of successful musicians do.

A life in music

Jennifer has a lot of control over her music. Her lyrics give her the chance to express her feelings. She sings about her life and events that have **inspired** her. 'Dear Ben' was dedicated to Ben Affleck. He and J. Lo were engaged at the time she wrote this song.

Spanish songs

J. Lo feels very strongly about her Puerto Rican background. She is proud to be Hispanic-American. Most of her songs are sung in English. Some are set to Spanish lyrics. In this way, Jennifer stays in touch with both her past and her present.

Chart success

Each of J. Lo's first four albums has sold millions of copies. Her third album was called *J. To Tha L-O!* This album was a **compilation** of **remixes**. It became the first remix album to go straight to the top of the US music charts.

A challenge

When asked why she was making an album, when she was already a successful actress, J. Lo replied: 'because it's tough, challenging and scary – all the stuff I love'.

Hip-hop star Ja Rule has worked with J. Lo on a number of her songs.

Changing names

The artist and producer Sean Combs has been known by many names, including P. Diddy, Puff Daddy and Puffy.

P. Diddy has worked with Mary J. Blige, R. Kelly, Mariah Carey and Jay-Z as well as J. Lo.

Working together

Jennifer has worked with some of the most respected and well-known people in the music industry. Together, they have created the hit music that has made J. Lo a music star.

Also featuring...

Many famous names from the world of hip-hop and R 'n' B have featured on J. Lo's songs. These include Marc Anthony, Ja Rule, Fat Joe and Big Punisher. These artists increase J. Lo's **credibility**. They have won J. Lo more fans.

Star words

20

credibility when people believe that someone is good at what they do

J. Lo performs with hip-hop star LL Cool J.

The producer

Music **producers** decide what a song sounds like. They work with the artist and the **sound engineers** to get the best possible music. When the recording is finished, they mix, tweak and adjust it until the song sounds just right. Two producers can make the same song sound totally different. J. Lo has worked with lots of producers. These include Emilio Estefan, Rodney Jerkins and Sean 'P. Diddy' Combs. Emilio Estefan's wife, Gloria Estefan, is another famous Hispanic pop star.

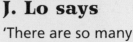

J. Lo says

'There are so many artists out there that I like and respect ... I have always thought about doing a duet with Craig David or Bono.'

J. Lo hopes to work with Craig David in the future.

★ Star fact

J. Lo's first album – *On the 6* – sold a million copies in just two months.

Star demands

This is what Jennifer allegedly demands wherever she goes:

a white dressing room
white flowers
white tables
white candles
seedless grapes
mineral water
a selection of music
Cuban food.

Touring and music videos

Jennifer Lopez toured as a dancer in the early 1990s. She has not yet done a full world tour in her own right. In 2001, however, she appeared on stage in Puerto Rico in front of thousands of fans. The show was later released on video.

Music videos

J. Lo's dance training prepared her perfectly for her music video performances, where she performs like a true professional. In 'I'm glad', she relived scenes from the hit 1980s film *Flashdance*. J. Lo is one of the most requested artists on the MTV music video channel.

The video of 'I'm glad' is based on the 1980s film *Flashdance*.

Star words   allegedly something that has been said, but not proved

Famous co-star

The most famous person to appear in one of J. Lo's music videos is Ben Affleck. He was seen laughing and joking with her in the video for 'Jenny from the block'.

The video for 'All I have' was shot in New York City.

J. Lo used to be one of Janet Jackson's dancers.

★ ★ ★ ★ ★ ★ ★ ★ ★ ★ ★

Janet's dancer

J. Lo has danced in music videos for other stars. She once danced in Janet Jackson's music video for 'That's the way love goes'. She was also in P. Diddy's video for 'Been around the world'.

★ ★ ★ ★ ★ ★ ★ ★ ★ ★ ★

Career highs

J. Lo presented Oscars to John Myhre and Gordon Sim for their work on the film *Chicago*.

Oscar night

At the Oscars in 2003, Jennifer presented the award for Best Art Direction. Being asked to present an Oscar is a great honour.

Jennifer Lopez's career has been full of dazzling moments. She is the most successful Hispanic-American actress ever. She has been **nominated** for acting awards. Her music has been extremely successful. Her films regularly top the **box-office takings**. The list goes on…

Doing the double

In 2001, Jennifer made history in the USA. She became the first woman to have a number one film and a number one album in the same week. The album was *J. Lo* and the film was *The Wedding Planner*, in which she starred with Matthew McConaughey.

Around the world

J. Lo is not just a star in her own country. She is a worldwide success. *J. Lo* also topped the charts around the world.

★ Star fact

Jennifer received US$2 million for her role in *Out of Sight* (1998). This meant she became the highest-paid Hispanic-American actress ever.

Star words

box-office takings how much money a film makes at the cinema

The album was number one in Argentina, Central America, Chile, Germany, Greece, Spain, Switzerland and her parents' home country – Puerto Rico.

Going up...

J. Lo's rising salary shows how her fame is increasing: *Selena* (1997): US$1million; *Out of Sight* (1998): US$2million; *The Wedding Planner* (2001): US$9million; *Maid in Manhattan* (2002): US$15million.

Matthew McConaughey and J. Lo starred in *The Wedding Planner*.

And the award goes to...

Between 1999 and 2003, J. Lo was **nominated** twelve times in the MTV music video awards.

J. Lo won MTV's award for Best Dance Video in 2000 for 'Waiting for tonight'.

A famous fan

In March 2002, one of J. Lo's biggest fans – Ben Affleck – decided to tell the world just how much he admired her. He paid for an advert in a magazine called The *Hollywood Reporter* that said: 'It has been nothing but an honor and a pleasure to work with you. I only wish I were lucky enough to be in all your movies.'

Fans

Millions of fans around the world have visited the cinema to see Jennifer Lopez on the **silver screen**. *Maid in Manhattan* has been one of her most popular films. In the US alone, it took almost US$94 million at the box office. *Anaconda* was her second most popular film, taking US$65.9 million.

> I don't ever think like I'm going to do this to win an award... I just hope that people like the music.

Premiere star

J. Lo always has time for her fans. At film **premieres**, she makes a big effort to meet the crowds. Jennifer spends a great deal of time speaking to fans and signing autographs. She also trys to answer questions that fans email to her website.

Around the world

J. Lo's first single, 'If you had my love', reached number one in more than 40 different countries around the world. Her official website has links to websites in 20 other countries. Japan is just one of the countries where J. Lo has fans.

J. Lo visited Tokyo, Japan, in February 2002. She was given a huge welcome.

Star words silver screen nickname for the large screen at the cinema

Jennifer signed lots of autographs at the UK premiere of *Maid in Manhattan*.

J. Lo's beauty tips

stay in shape

eat right

get plenty of rest

drink lots of water

J. Lo

Perhaps Jennifer's greatest **tribute** to her fans is her nickname – J. Lo. She saw banners decorated with 'J. Lo' when she sang on stage and decided to use the name herself. 'They [the fans] gave me a nickname that was actually pretty cool,' she says.

tribute act that shows feelings of respect or admiration towards someone

Style and image

If you are a pop star or a film star, image can be very important. Looking good is part of the job. J. Lo is as famous for looking good as she is for her work. When she was young, J.Lo did not have much money. She used to make her own outfits from old sweatshirts and jogging outfits.

Inspiration

J. Lo is now **inspired** by many different **cultures** and styles. One video had a Latin-American theme, with **flamenco** dancing and clothing. However, Jennifer is just as comfortable in jeans.

New images

Changing her clothes allows J. Lo to change her image. In her videos and when she is performing, J. Lo often wears cool, sassy outfits. When she **promotes** her films she wears clothes that are classy and elegant. At the London **premiere** of *Maid in Manhattan*, she looked **sophisticated** in a full-length dress.

" I know what it's like to work 9 to 5 and have dreams of a better life. "

Jennifer looked amazing at the UK premiere of *Maid in Manhattan*.

Star words   sophisticated stylish and elegant

Her figure

Many Hollywood actresses feel the pressure to be very thin, but not Jennifer Lopez. Although dancing and exercise keep her fit and toned, she still has a very curvy figure. J. Lo is totally happy with the way she looks – it is part of who she is.

★ ★ ★ ★ ★ ★ ★ ★ ★ ★

Changing image

J. Lo likes to try out different looks. Sometimes she wears vests and jeans. Sometimes she wears stylish, slinky outfits. Whatever she wears, it is often in the newspapers the next day.

★ ★ ★ ★ ★ ★ ★ ★ ★ ★

J. Lo looked stylish promoting *Maid in Manhattan* in Paris.

J. Lo looks cool on stage.

29

The scent of success

Jennifer has her own perfume and cosmetics. The 'Glow' range was launched in 2002. The perfume, shower gel and body lotion are very popular.

A billboard displays one of J. Lo's fashion advertisements.

Exploiting her image

Important events, such as the Oscars, give fashion designers the chance to show off their designs. They often ask famous actresses to wear their outfits. J. Lo often goes to celebrity events wearing dresses by famous designers. It is good **publicity** for her and for the designer, too.

Cover girl

Jennifer does not need to sing, dance or act to make money. Her cover-girl good looks sell a whole range of products. She is a **spokesperson** for a **cosmetics** company. In 2003, a French company announced that she would be modelling their bags and jewellery.

> " I wanted it to be fresh, I wanted it to be clean. (J. Lo on 'Glow') "

REGENCY

Star words

exploit to take advantage of someone or something
spokesperson someone who represents a company

J. Lo the label

In 2001, Jennifer Lopez launched her own fashion line. She works with her design team to produce girls' and women's clothes and accessories for the J. Lo label. The products are funky and up-to-date – just like Jennifer!

Star fact

Jennifer Lopez sponsors a girls' soccer team from the Bronx. The J. Lo Girls are aged between 11 and 13 years old. They wear strips supplied by J. Lo herself!

J. Lo's new range of clothes was launched at a store in New York, USA.

In April 2002, Natalie Martinez won the J. Lo model search.

J. Lo's models

Thousands of young women **auditioned** to model the J. Lo fashion collection. The winner, Natalie Martinez, was from Miami, USA.

Personal interests

★ ★ ★ ★ ★ ★ ★ ★ ★ ★

Miami

J. Lo says: 'My favourite place to vacation is Miami. I recently purchased a house there and can't spend enough time there. I love the weather...'

★ ★ ★ ★ ★ ★ ★ ★ ★ ★

Many celebrities spend time in Miami Beach, Florida.

J. Lo has a very busy schedule of filming and recording. She travels the world going to film **premieres** and award ceremonies. She also **promotes** her music, clothes and perfume. Jennifer has very little spare time. When she does have some time off, she enjoys relaxing in one of her homes.

"J. Lo is often seen wearing expensive jewellery. 'I like the bling bling', she says."

Keeping fit

Jennifer likes to keep in shape. She spends time at the dance studio. She learns new steps and practises **routines**. She also works out regularly. Gunnar Peterson is one of the top Hollywood personal trainers. He makes sure that she keeps fit.

Star words bling bling shiny, expensive, trendy things

No place like home

Jennifer has a hilltop mansion in Beverly Hills, Los Angeles. She has another mansion on Miami Beach. In Georgia, she owns an island on which she has yet another mansion.

J. Lo loves to shop.

Shopping

Jennifer Lopez knows how to earn money. She also knows how to spend it! She once struggled to get by on her dancer's wage. Now she is famous for her shopping trips. She gives expensive gifts to her friends and family. In 1997, she earned US$1 million for her role in *Selena*. One of the first things she bought was a brand-new car for her mother. She bought an Aston Martin for Ben Affleck in 2002.

J. Lo's mansion in Beverly Hills, Los Angeles, is fit for a pop queen.

Film stars including Nicole Kidman eat at J. Lo's restaurant.

Other roles

Jennifer Lopez has many business interests. Her **production** company is called Nuyorican Productions. It makes films and television shows. J. Lo plans to co-produce and star in some of these. The company **promotes** drama, comedy, reality shows, music and dance.

J. Lo's nightclub

J. Lo invested in a nightclub in Los Angeles. It is called The Conga Room. It opened in February 1998. It is run by J. Lo's first husband, Ojani Noa and is very popular. Local and South American musicians perform there regularly. Visitors can even take dancing lessons there!

Madre's menu

The menu at J. Lo's restaurant includes Cuban meals. You could have *picadillo oriental* – beef cooked with olives and served in a sweet potato basket. Or you could try *pastelon* – a beef and **plantain** casserole.

J. Lo's restaurant

In April 2002, J. Lo opened her own restaurant in Pasadena, California. Yet again, Jennifer showed how proud she is of her family and her roots. The restaurant was named Madre's, after the Spanish word for 'mother'. It serves Cuban and Puerto Rican food. When she opened her restaurant, her guests included actors Nicole Kidman, Christian Slater and Brooke Shields, and US talk show host Jay Leno.

> "She works very hard and I respect her for that. (Hip-hop star Ja Rule)"

Star words plantain type of banana

The new Carmen

Jennifer likes new challenges. One project that she wants to work on is *Carmen*. She is keen to make a modern film version of George Bizet's famous **opera**. J. Lo plans to **produce** the film and play the leading role.

J. Lo visited the building site of her restaurant to make sure everything was going well.

★ ★ ★ ★ ★ ★ ★ ★ ★ ★ ★

Carmen

J. Lo loves the story of *Carmen*. It is about a beautiful gypsy woman. Don José is a prison guard who loves Carmen. When she commits a crime, Don José helps her to escape from prison. Later he sees Carmen with another man and kills her.

★ ★ ★ ★ ★ ★ ★ ★ ★ ★ ★

Carmen is a dramatic and exciting opera.

Media spotlight

The shooting

J. Lo and P. Diddy's relationship broke down. Their break-up is often blamed on the **infamous** events of 27 December 1999. The couple were at a New York nightclub when shots were fired. P. Diddy was charged with gun possession. He was later cleared of the charges, but he and Jennifer split up.

Since the 1990s, J. Lo has become very famous. She has also had some **high-profile** relationships. These have brought her even more **publicity**. This **media** attention has made her personal life difficult.

The waiter

J. Lo's first husband was a waiter called Ojani Noa. He proposed during the party to celebrate the end of filming on *Selena*. Jennifer accepted. The marriage lasted just a year.

> ❝ I didn't think about everything that came along with (fame). I lost my anonymity, privacy. ❞

P. Diddy and J. Lo were one of the coolest showbiz couples.

Star words **media** ways of communicating with lots of people, such as television, radio and newspaper

J. Lo married Ojani Noa in 1997.

★ ★ ★ ★ ★ ★ ★ ★ ★

Divorces

Celebrity marriage breakdowns are common. They are often caused by the pressures of fame. Drew Barrymore was divorced twice before she was 27. Elvis Presley's daughter, Lisa Marie, was divorced three times by the age of 34.

★ ★ ★ ★ ★ ★ ★ ★ ★

The rapper

Jennifer's next boyfriend really caught the attention of the public and the **paparazzi**. P. Diddy is a respected rap artist. He was one of the **producers** on J. Lo's first album. She starred in his music videos. They made a glamorous couple, but their relationship lasted for only seventeen months.

Fashion designer Donatella Versace threw a wedding party for J. Lo and Cris Judd in Italy.

The dancer

Soon after, Jennifer found love once again. Cris Judd was one of the backing dancers on her video for 'My love don't cost a thing'. J. Lo promoted Cris to be her **choreographer**. They were married on 29 September 2001 in a lavish ceremony. The relationship did not last very long, however. The couple divorced the next year.

paparazzi photographers who follow celebrities in order to take pictures of them

Celebrity couples

Many famous acting couples have worked together like J. Lo and Ben Affleck. Nicole Kidman and Tom Cruise co-starred in *Days of Thunder* and *Far and Away*. Brad Pitt was in an episode of *Friends* with his wife Jennifer Aniston.

★ ★ ★ ★ ★ ★ ★ ★ ★ ★ ★

Brad Pitt and Jennifer Aniston are another celebrity couple.

Ben Affleck

Jennifer Lopez met Ben Affleck on the set of *Gigli* in 2001. Ben was very impressed with Jennifer's personality and acting ability. He put a full-page advertisement in The *Hollywood Reporter*, to say how much he had enjoyed working with her.

Jennifer and Ben enjoyed watching the LA Lakers play basketball.

Jen and Ben

Gigli flopped at the box office, but the romance between Ben and Jennifer grew. They made another film together – *Jersey Girl*. They became engaged in 2002. During a television interview the couple **sensationally** announced that they were getting married.

To wed...

By 2003, **media** interest in Jennifer Lopez and Ben Affleck had gone crazy. The couple were photographed wherever they went. There were lots of rumours about their wedding. They wanted the marriage to be private, so the couple tried to fool the press.

> " What should have been a joyful and sacred day could be spoiled for us, our families and our friends. "

Star words   sensational something surprising and exciting

...or not to wed?

They pretended that they were getting married in Hawaii. They hired 'decoy brides' to draw attention away from themselves. Details were leaked that the wedding would actually be in Santa Barbara, California. Jennifer and Ben decided that they had had enough. They postponed and later cancelled the wedding. Shortly after that they split up.

★ Star fact

J. Lo received a pink diamond engagement ring from Ben Affleck. It was said to be worth over US$1 million.

★ ★ ★ ★ ★ ★ ★ ★ ★ ★ ★

Rose petals

Ben Affleck's marriage proposal was very romantic. He surprised Jennifer by filling a house with rose petals. Candles glowed on every stair. One of her songs was playing in the background. Then he asked her to marry him.

★ ★ ★ ★ ★ ★ ★ ★ ★ ★ ★

J. Lo and Ben Affleck drew the crowds when they went to the **premiere** of Ben's film *Daredevil*.

decoy someone who pretends to be someone else, in order to fool people

Will J. Lo and Will star together?

Wait and see

There are always rumours in the **media** and on the Internet about J. Lo's next projects. Jennifer is rumoured to be appearing in a thriller called *Tick Tock*, a musical with Robert de Niro, and a romantic comedy with Will Smith. Will any of these films reach cinema screens?

The future for J. Lo

Jennifer always has a lot of offers for work. This means that she can pick and choose the films she wants to work on. Ever since she played the lead role in *Selena*, she has been constantly busy. Film companies know that audiences will want to go to see Jennifer Lopez, whether she is playing the part of a dance teacher, a maid or a single mother.

Back on the dance floor

One of Jennifer's most recent films is called *Shall We Dance?* Richard Gere is her co-star. He plays an accountant from Chicago who works too hard. The film gives J. Lo the chance to dance again. She plays a dance teacher who helps to brighten up Gere's life by giving him dance lessons.

Cartoon character

Jennifer is in no danger of being **typecast** any time soon. She has been linked with a film called *Shrink!* This story is based on an Internet comic strip by Rob Liefeld. It was announced that Jennifer would play the part of a superhero **psychiatrist** in love with good and bad superheroes.

 **Star fact**

Rob Liefeld, creator of *Shrink!*, talked about J. Lo's character in the film: 'She's not going to get dressed up in **spandex**... She gets to look great in her designer clothes...'

Star words

psychiatrist someone who treats people with mental illness

Robert Redford has been a film star since the 1960s.

Oscar time?

In *An Unfinished Life*, J. Lo co-stars with Robert Redford. This is a serious film. Some people thought this would be Jennifer's chance for an Oscar.

An Unfinished Life

In this film, Jennifer plays a widow who is down on her luck. She moves in with her father-in-law, who she has not seen for some time. He lives on a ranch in Wyoming. This drama is very different from her romantic comedies like *Maid in Manhattan* and *The Wedding Planner*.

Jersey Girl was the second film in which J. Lo and Ben Affleck starred together. This scene was filmed in Central Park, New York City.

Family time

Family is important to J. Lo. She says, 'I come from a great, loving family, and one day I would like the same thing.'

★ ★ ★ ★ ★ ★ ★ ★ ★ ★

Jennifer is close to her father and the rest of her family.

What's next?

Although J. Lo spent much of 2003 on film **sets**, she plans to return to the recording studio. It has been reported that her next album will contain pop and R 'n' B material, like J. Lo's previous chart-toppers. Will a world tour be announced?

J. Lo – the brand

Jennifer's many business interests are going from strength to strength. A range of J. Lo jewellery has been designed. The collections of clothes with the J. Lo label are selling well. Film stars Natalie Portman and Kirsten Dunst have both been seen wearing clothes from the J. Lo range.

Media interest

J. Lo is one of the most famous people in the world. Every move she makes is photographed, filmed, and written about. Everyone wants to know what she will do next.

Third time lucky?

In June 2004 J.Lo suprised the media. She married Latin singing star Marc Anthony at her home in Los Angeles. J.Lo and Marc had been able to keep their relationship away from the media.Their quiet wedding involved only 40 guests.Will this third marriage work out for J.Lo? One thing is certain – she and Marc will not be able to avoid media attention for long!

Jennifer enjoys acting with children. This picture is from *Maid in Manhattan*.

J. Lo is photographed wherever she goes.

Doing it all

'... I love what I do. I have a passion for the work, it's not about being famous. At the beginning, I started to dance because I love to dance. Then I sang because I loved to sing and act because I loved to act. It's very fulfilling to me and I'd be doing it even if I weren't famous. I'd be doing it somewhere.'

Find out more

Books to read

Galaxy of Superstars: Jennifer Lopez, Anne E. Hill (Chelsea House Publications, 2000)

Jennifer Lopez, Trevor Baker (Carlton Books, 2001)

Latinos in the Limelight: Jennifer Lopez, Leah Furman (Chelsea House Publications, 2001)

Penguin Readers: Level 1: Jennifer Lopez, R. Martin (Longman, 2000)

Music video

Let's Get Loud (February 2003)

Filmography

American Darlings (due 2005)
Bordertown (due 2005)
Monster-in-Law (2005)
An Unfinished Life (2005)
Shall We Dance (2004)
Jersey Girl (2004)
Gigli (2003)
Maid in Manhattan (2002)
Enough (2002)
Angel Eyes (2001)
The Wedding Planner (2001)
The Cell (2000)
Antz (1998)
Out of Sight (1998)
U-Turn (1997)
Anaconda (1997)
Selena (1997)

Blood and Wine (1997)
Jack (1996)
Money Train (1995)
My Family (1995)
My Little Girl (1986)

Discography
Rebirth (March 2005)
This is Me... Then (November 2002)
J To Tha L-O! The Remixes (February 2002)
J. Lo (July 2001)
On the 6 (July 1999)

Websites
J. Lo's official website is:
http://www.jenniferlopez.com
This official site has details of J. Lo
merchandise: **http://www.shopjlo.com**
Another good music website is:
http://www.bbc.co.uk/totp

Disclaimer
All the Internet addresses (URLs) given in this book were valid at the
time of going to press. However, due to the dynamic nature of the
Internet, some addresses may have changed, or sites may have ceased
to exist since publication. While the author, packager and publishers
regret any inconvenience this may cause readers, no responsibility for
any such changes can be accepted by either the author, packager or
the publishers.

Glossary

allegedly something that has been said, but not proved

ambition having something you want to achieve. An ambitious person wants to achieve something.

anonymity when no one knows who you are

audition interview for a musician or actor, where they show their skills

bling bling shiny, expensive, trendy things

box-office takings how much money a film makes at the cinema

choreographer person who makes up dance routines for pop videos and live performances

compilation CD that includes songs from different sources

cosmetics beauty products such as make-up

credibility when people believe that someone is good at what they do

cultures people from different countries and races

debut someone's first appearance in a new role

decoy someone who pretends to be someone else, in order to fool people

director person in charge of making a film

exclusive high-class and expensive

exploit to take advantage of someone or something

flamenco lively type of Spanish dancing

high-profile something that is often in the news

immigrant someone who has come to live in a new country

infamous well known for the wrong reasons

inspired getting ideas from people or things

martial arts types of self-defence or attack, such as judo or karate

media ways of communicating with lots of people, such as television, radio and newspaper

nominated to be put forward as one of the right people to win an award

on location if a film is shot outside a film studio, this is said to be 'on location'

opera play that is set to music

paparazzi photographers who follow celebrities in order to take pictures of them

plantain type of banana

premiere first showing of a film, often with celebrities invited

produce (film) film producers organize the people and the money to make a film

produce (music) when a song is produced, this includes arranging and mixing the music

promote tell people about a new product

psychiatrist someone who treats people with mental illness

publicity when someone is noticed by the public

remixes new versions of an original recording

role part that an actor plays in a film, play or television show

routine set of practised dance moves

salsa type of Latin-American music and dance

sensational something surprising and exciting

set part of a film studio where a film is shot

silver screen nickname for the large screen at the cinema

sit-com short for situation comedy. This is a TV comedy show that has the same places and characters each week

sophisticated stylish and elegant

sound engineers people who record the music in a studio

spandex shiny and tight-fitting fabric

spokesperson someone who represents a company

strive work very hard

tribute act that shows feelings of respect or admiration towards a famous performer or performers

typecast when an actor is given very similar roles to play, over and over again

unique one of a kind

Index